Maria Papageorgiou-Foroudi

The Fading Garden

HAMPSTEAD PRESS

© 2021 Maria Papageorgiou-Foroudi

This book is copyright. Except for private study, research, criticism or reviews, as permitted under the Copyright Act, no part of this book may be reproduced, stored in a retrieval system or transmitted in any form or by any means without prior written permission. Enquiries should be made to the publisher.

First published 2021 by Hampstead Press
hampsteadpress@outlook.com

ISBN: 978-0-6452885-0-6

All Rights Reserved

Also by Maria Papageorgiou-Foroudi

VSS365 Anthology: Volume One: A stunning collection of Very Short Stories from Around the Globe (contributor)

Tears In My Bread (Australian Scholarly Publishing, 2020)

Table of Contents

Egg 1
Angry Man 2
Kite Flying 3
Accident in The Valley 4
The New School Year 5
Visitation 6
Body 7
Moving 8
Cataract 9
The Crane at Rest 10
A Family Drive to Bright 11
Quills 12
The Street 13
At Rest 15
Kintsugi 17
Flowers 18
Journey To The Centre 19
Flow 20
Carlton 21
Emancipation 22
Nightmare 24
Plum Tree 25
Garden Party 26
St Kilda, 11 pm 27
Cycle 28

Indigo	29
Looking Out	30
Milkbar	31
Disability	32
Urban Paradise	34
Memories of The Playground	35
Looking for Home	36
Low	37
Bushfire	38
Imperfection	39
Hot Springs	40
Housework	41
Aged Care	42
Enrichment Classes	43
Lemon	44
Lock	45
Neighbour	46
Evening Ritual	48
Orchid	49
Local Park	50
Inspiration	52
A Trip to the Beach	53
The Merri Creek	54
Indolence	55
The Park At Night	56
The Shower	57
Stillborn	58
Suicide	59

No-Man's Land 60
Risk Taker 61
Retro-Movie 62
Watching Fall 64
Letters 65
Summer Gluttony 66
Tomato 67
Exercise 68
My Parents Sitting on the Verandah 70
Lighting The Barbeque 71
Voyage 72
Birthing Tree 73
Paradise 74
Name 75
Midden 76
Coming Home 77
Mists 78
About the Author 79

'The gates of hell are open night and day; Smooth the descent, and easy is the way: But to return, and view the cheerful skies, in this the task and mighty labour lies.'

Virgil, The Aeneid

Egg

For days the chickens squabbled in the yard
Torn feathers revealing skin as pink as a newborn's:
The pecking order disturbed by the new one, though there was no escape
Since their wings were clipped by the shearing scissors to stop them
Flying on top of the outside dunny and the ancient fig tree.

The cold winter made the neighbours grumble
About the noise in the coop:
And soon a plate was filled with six or seven yolks,
Some small, some large,
Speckled with bloodspots swimming in a white mucus sea,
Placed in the fridge,
Shell-less and plucked straight from the red isthmus
Like yellow and orange boats.

I inspected them closely with disgust and admiration,
Noting their sulfurous beauty, as bright as saffron
And thick with layered secrets of flight and creation,
Bulbous and fresh like a garland of
Swollen planets, the yard silent for once, the neighbours sated
While the chicken shit fertilised the growing beans which
Started to spread over the stakes.

I think about that aged silence over the din of morning traffic, wondering
If death is the microscope which magnifies virtue.

Waiting at the lights on Banksia Street,
I watch feathers falling from the packed crates lining the truck,
The death rattle of agitated clucking,
The truck returning empty and serene within the hour.

Angry Man

The man across the street is angry again;
We've heard the doors slam like hands against the frame
And the engine revving in the driveway,
Smoke rising from the bull nostrils of the bonnet,
The brake and accelerator both clamped down hard,
The wheels turn again and again
Like bald black sunflowers, their corolla
Shaved with heat.

It's a warning for the rest of us to retreat and watch through the windows:
We see the woman crouch between the fence, low down like a rabbit
Her eyes microscopic with salt behind the thick glasses:
She listens through the blades of grass which remind her of green cables
And reads messages scratched into once wet blocks of footpath
'B loves T'
While the police pick evidence from the boot into clear plastic bags,
Collecting syringes and weed and spoons and filling in the log.
She waits for them to fold the man away into an unlatched box
Of intervention orders, cells and
Rehab courses.

A couple of days later we see them again, holding hands
And buckets of Dulux,
Painting the front fence that wobbles and peels out the front.
Squinting, she laughs at something he says as he finishes the monologue
Which has captured her for at least ten minutes.

I notice that her glasses are in his pocket
The lens round like the wheel.

Kite Flying

There is a spot in Royal Park where the nylon birds
Play off the fingers of girls and boys who guide them like puppet masters,
Under the winter sun and the screen of a billowing stratus.
The plastic spine bends and folds at the mercy of a winter wind which
Smells of rain, the kite blowing as high as the windows which reflect
The theatre's lights at the hospital nearby.

The master stands with a light smile,
Conquering the air with the unfurled white spider webs which stick in
The breeze as we finally reach the spot.
The wind rushes from the trees as I shake the kite like a dusty
Rag, hoping for flight, hoping to send it into the empty space above us
Which rocks with the morning shuffle of joggers and
Leadless dogs, and the ghosts of girls murdered, stones placed
On their faces by long-haired men
Who murmur spells.

But no matter how many times we try,
The earth caves in on our hands like a dead rainbow,
A woman holding an open suitcase walks past wailing:

The kite collects mud under the wet sky.

Accident in The Valley

By the time our bike pedals take us close to the scene
An ambulance wail is already piercing the wave of our sprint:
The car's nose is folded like a sucked cigarette
Into the ashtray of the tree, a few puffs of
Smoke blowing off the paint and into
The burnt grass beyond.

The birds have fled over the farmer's house and the walnut farm,
Heading toward the river.

The man's eyes are open. He says nothing.
His pupils rapidly fill the room of his
Eye like a slow wave,
Like a coffee cup filling or a
Mouth opening to a lover's nipple: And a tiny ribbon of blood
Trickles from his mouth like a spear, the lips
Twitching towards a smile.
I could imagine him reclining on a lounge chair,
If it wasn't for the adrenaline being rocketed into his arm,
And the plastic wrappers of the syringe blowing around.

While they open his shirt to place cords on the white skin
I look around, and the smell of mountain flowers pour
Off my nose.
The push on his chest marries with the hits of the horse's hoof.
Behind us, nightfall blooms over the valley

The New School Year

The school year began with a funeral:

The children's mouths pressed silent of chats and tall stories
Ushered in by diplomats in teacher's hats, the principal gowned
In her grimmest face:

Past the peeling statue with its outstretched arms
Clothed in baby blue and vacant black eyes,
The silver trolley groaning with the weight of the old woman.

Not that any of the children knew her name-
Who was she anyway?
They pondered and sweated in February's heat on the flat pews,
Twisting new shoes into the gaps of the wood, cut of the same wood
As the coffin, conjuring fictions of what must later be confessed
Through the flyscreen, bearing false witness in order to gain a Hail Mary,
While the priest breathed whiskey amens onto the silver microphone.

The service wore on as the funeral director swore under his moustache:
The teacher's gossip looping past the unpolished cups and garish capes
Which hung still in the vestry

Visitation

Though we waited for the autopsy
He was never more alive than in the bowl of fruit on the bench:
The pomegranate which had slowly roughened into red leather in the
Humidity of late summer, selected only days earlier by
His hand at the Queen Victoria markets,
Its red blood spotting the floor as we spliced
The yellow chambers, drifting up from the long silence
And dented couches to feed the body,
Walking between the fill and drain of memory and daze.

And when we stepped into the yard, his singlet still lapped
The breeze on the clothesline:
The one which hid the splinters of artery days earlier
Under the cover of its fabric.

We sat stunned on the grass, staring at the empty space between
And around

Body

Though I tried to believe this body was my own,
There was a certain comfort
In the myopia that came during the years of discovery, my sight
Measured in fractions by optometrists in dark rooms, when the blur of
Arms and head was confusing enough to make the form seem unique.

The image came into sharper focus as I aged,
Watching my hands grip the pram
As my father's knotted fingers gripped his silver walking frame,
Stubbornly holding onto whatever was left of his vertical stance after the
Hard shifts of production lines and illiteracy.

And there above us: the glinting framed testamurs
And showroom-worthy vehicles rested
Like purring sated cats in the warmth,
The handsome children on the couch competing with each other in a game,
The symmetry of their faces mathematically drafted.

I readjust the glasses on my nose, and move closer to the mirror;
His face looks back, my hands hold ropes of gold;
His hands clutch an empty suitcase:

My reflection is overwhelmed.

Moving

The removalists strip the house with the efficiency of an
Undertaker:
All sorry eyes and carbon copy invoices
As they coil entrails of curtains and bookshelves
Into the back of the van,
Bandaging the bed with soft plastic wrap after they
Carelessly crack the plaster on the way out.

It takes a while for me to drop the key into the open mouth
Of the mailbox once they'd gone;
That small thin metal fingerprint which had hung from my neck
On the long metal umbilicus those nine years,
Caked with pieces of sultana and sweat and the crumbs
Of school runs and market shopping.

The cobwebs hang from the eye of the window like
Silver knots and I check the door again,
Just to make sure it's locked- you can never be too sure.
And turning to the car I catch my jumper against the swing
That hangs on the tree, waving its rope in the spit of rain.

How long has this been here? I say, stalling.
Remember when Alex tried to fly off it and broke his arm?

And the children laugh and point
As a nest of brown strands from my hairbrush,
Plucked under the sun of many mornings,
Is knitted by a noisy miner on the hedge.

Cataract

At some point the hate that had grown too heavy has drifted
Upward from our stomachs and spleens like a tumour,
Making its way to our mouth,
Hate-spittle thudding into telephones
And keyboards and the fleshy bars
Of bystander's ears.

Lava of the tongue
Becomes a hard disc that covers the eye:
A mosaic of splinter-memories stuck fast
Like a fork in jelly,
The lens silently slipping to the underworld beneath the feet
Strangled by Persephone's protein plaits.

In blindness we attain a certain amount of relief:
Knowing there was never any comfort anyway
In spring's plastic lens.

The Crane at Rest

It took a plague to swipe the metal arm of the crane:
The one which hooked and lifted with wire ropes and sheaves,
A giant's fishing rod suspended over our heads, dangling
Glass eyes into the blind walls of city buildings

Its sharp tickle was inside the shirt-strapped throat every morning;
Slicing the flesh with its huge fat finger,
The metal nail slipping clean down the middle of the trachea
Until all we felt was the bile rising as the shark-toothed escalators
Of Parliament and Flagstaff Stations spat their
Steps at us.

Later the scales rip quietly from the skin,
Under the dark elm of the suburbs.
We float face down
In the brackish water of the small pond.
Time has shown the promise to be false:

The fish opens its gills in gasp,
The shadow breaks the backbone like a
Stick.

A Family Drive to Bright

We spin down the road leading to the town in the black car
Which blows like the bloated felt of an angry cloud.
The children are fighting and pulling each other's hair
In the backseat
While in the front, we silently drown out the kaleidoscope
Of small houses with inflatable Santas and cafes and
Tin roofs as green as switch and pumpkin seed.
Our eyes catch the occasional image of a fluff of lamb resting under
Its mother.

The hand grows tense on the wheel

Later we limp into the driveway on the burnt lip of the mountain,
The hot wheels shooing away the grey of kangaroo and the tiny
Rabbits that tease the bushes.
Food comes in Styrofoam, leaking through the bag
After a half-hour wait in a perfectly spaced line,
Burning rectangle marks on our legs.

We each take turns staring at the hills beyond as we
Mash the food with dry mouths,
Later taking the telescope on the deck to our face:
Swallowing the starbursts which fill the vastness
Of the pines beyond, stacks of logs
Packed like severed giant's legs
On the bed of a city-bound truck.

Quills

Once, cinnamon birds had turned the evening sky green
With their majestic tails:
Scraping fragrant quills of spice off the trunk,
They knitted nests which smelt of hot tea.

By morning, plucked feathers stabbed writer's ink jars,
And the sliced tree lay quietly in the mill.

The Street

A woman kneels on her lawn
Hovering above the green blades with the greatest concentration
As if it were a magic carpet with a loose thread:
Her thick gardening gloves are neatly placed beside her
One on top of the other as if joined in prayer
Trimming the irregular heads with a blunt scissor
A huge bucket beside her.

Further down the street an old man wears
A kitchen towel over his head,
Painting the yellow-leaved lemon tree
With thick strokes of lime.
Can't he see that his Ford is trampling a group of iris heads
Which dangle like roadkill under the wheel?

It's a late afternoon in Spring.

The Ivanhoe street is dotted with pre-war squat homes,
Victorian verandas with bathtubs and benches on polished decks and
The gold heart above is ticking towards dusk:
A cluster of birds starts to sing in the eucalypt above the powerline
Spontaneously, without reason,
Their calls flapping over the wire fence,
Two or three cherries hanging off branches
Like dehydrated heads on pikes.

At some point the old man and the woman will straighten their backs
And stand up,
Wordlessly admiring their garden:
They will place their tools aside and walk into the house
Slipping out of their shoes in the hallway

As they have many times before.
And the birds will sing once more, as if to say:

'Here is the secret: this is how to make the sun set'

At Rest

We are surprised by the cemetery on our afternoon walk;
A small mouth of green flecked with
Grey tombstones,
Splitting the jaw of houses and tidy gardens on Hawdon Street;
A silent scream of Hade's gates
Between pools and trampolines and the sunny voices of
Newsreaders which tremble beneath slabs of screens.

Evergreen where there is rot and bone below,
Prickly candles shooting from precise branches
In whorls and Fibonacci codes
And the cones could well be miniature
Candelabras in their thousands
Which break like globes over sleeping heads
Lying in damaged boxes:
Some are in threads of suits
Hastily organized by distracted widows;
And others draped in the cotton of the nursery
Mouths half sealed with undertaker's glue,
Their feet pointed in every direction of the compass.

Some of the stones are bent far forwards as if by the force
Of a heavy hand which has pushed them aside
In a quest to escape:
Others are mossy with neglect,
The words barely perceptible through the cracks.
Yet the stories that lie beneath them
Pull at my hem:
It is here that an eleven-year-old girl has been lying
For over one hundred years,

Her ear cast to the ground,
Listening to the call of the distant school bell.

The roots silently strangle the chaotic blanket
Of dust and fat, the cheers of the footballers falling
Loudly across the road, bouncing hard off the silence.

Kintsugi

A puzzle holds beauty in the unique curve and print
Of each piece – it is not seen as broken or defective.
Yet the broom has worn thin, becoming a gnarled
Brush, and our back curves with effort as we sweep
The specks and counters into the dustpan, each
Ground strike pointing toward a gutter,
Bleeding its plastic death into the mouth of
The sea;
For the shattered specks and slices are what the broken
Man refuses to see, there is no kintsugi here.

He can search for completeness under bright lights,
But would he see it:
The leg held aloft by the fixation device,
Gracefully extended as if in dance, a scalpel and drill biting into
The wet bloody crack, titanium filling the breach,
The head of the screw and the arm of the bracket embracing
The gape of the bone,
The masked artist breathing life into what you
Would have folded into the bin.

Over the months the bone and metal meet,
The strength of a titan forming, those pre-Olympian savages
In the humble shoe.

What lies below the scarlet ribbon of the stitches
Excites the metal detector (at least it understands)
And makes the security guards scramble and stand
At its voiceless command.

Flowers

Bunches of flowers bathed in chemicals recline like toxic Cleopatras
Absorbing monitor and morphine, occasionally dangling from
The bruise of a bride's hand

I tell you the dead only belong with the dead:

Painted yellow and orange as if by a mortician's heavy brush,
Dainty petals lay dead in their plastic sheet
Wrapped with white paper to stop the ugly seep of fluids
Tearing down sleeves,
Wound up and presented like a stillborn
With a garish ribbon on its head:

The only truth on this painted corpse
Is on the stem: a thorn to test your reflexes,
A needle to remind you you're alive.

Journey To The Centre

The wheels of the taxi seem to prevaricate
Around the twists of mountain and
Roadside icons which gape at us:
Their bottles of oil next to burnt wicks
Which once blazed for the dead

For hours we slide on the back of the green and black snake
That leads to Delphi
Finally reaching the head with its treasuries and holy rocks
And Pythia's chair: now empty of her tangled tongue which
Rolled high on ethylene, not far from the empty tourist shops
Where foreign-cast statuettes are sold by
Rapacious shop keepers, priced separately for the sun-stroked tourist:
So much cheaper if you muster the right
Accent

Later we move toward the sphynx which beckons blindly from the
Museum's stage,
High on its pedestal, riddle-less, staring through its white eye,
Next to the charioteer whose hands are empty of reigns.
The navel has stretched like a slash over the stomach
Up here in these hills,
But to wonder about this seems to displease the gods:
And the freckle nosed child that dances and laughs noisily,
Much too close to the edge of Parnassus
Impales himself on the fang of the peak.

Flow

There is no need to dab the eye with a tissue when the tear falls,
Or to hide the red flow between the legs with the bleached
Tube of toxic shock that enters
Like a white finger,

There is no need to halt salt under the arms with aluminium strokes,
Hushing words with a heavy pat which shaves the scalp,
Muzzling the awful beauty of amniotic sacs
Bursting on grocery store floors.

Flow is the road which peels like black sticky tape
To the source: of hot car seats and the static of
Forced conversations which lead to the cataract gorge and waterfall,
Splashing into the lake from a wooden swing which is laced around
An ancient eucalypt and
Fountains of Apollo whose sculpted limbs
Spurt water past carefully averted horse's heads.

Sunbeams bounce
Hard onto the sheaf and the windmill
Burns the air as it spins:
The grind of the millstone winds itself into a frenzy
As it throws the flour to the ground

Carlton

Who knows where I will find some silence to press my ear to today:
A 'For Lease' sign dangles over restaurant tables that now accommodate
Patrons of flies and dust,
And a moped purrs down Rathdowne Street,
Its small black wheels whiskering the ground past the library
And the park.

Somewhere beyond the crescent of the mosque with its
Yellow caterpillar of taxis the cemetery claims the block with its
Green fence,
Polyester garlands around the cold necks of its bars and
Cautionary signs which warn of uneven terrain
And falling bodies.

It has been raining all morning and a white sun is waking
From behind grey sheets, curiosity leading me to read
The one-page storybooks which blend numbers and dates,
Verses that hang silent while the hero
Rests with a silent mouth below.

A maintenance car screams down the path lined
With mud and the stare of photos picked in fogs of grief.
It slows when it sees me, the driver widening his eyes at the near miss:
Only the suspicious-eyed cleaner and I
Exist here,
Though beyond the fence, bells of cycles scratch the air.

I rush past the exit sign toward the sounds of cars and trams,
Past the grave whose slab has cracked like a heart.

Emancipation

Every second year we fly toward lands
Which exhale heat through nostrils of temples and thrones, places where
Kings once stood in towers, watching oars
Stir the water, gathering the sea in
Their robes

We imagine the boy's schoolroom
And what his fine sandals must have looked like,
Olympia's ghost dreaming of greatness as his feet hit the spurs,
Past the soot of the blacksmith which taps
Through the maim of Hephaestus,
Leaving Pella's walls to
Gallop as far as the Indus

To the west lies a cotton field:
And when the bus stops
And the tourists are preparing their cameras
A ball somehow blows its way between my feet.
As the others bend to read inscriptions,
I genuflect toward the white grandmother head,
Stunned awake by its green spiky ear pricking my hand,
Grasping the embryo of the cloak
Just as the Africans did, picking until their fingers were
Raw, first the globe passing between the gin,
Later the thread through the charkha.

This escaped cloud of stick and seed will not be snapped on the loom.
For once it has refused to become a thread of emancipation,

Freeing itself from the dizziness of the wheel.
Has it heard the wail of the soldiers blow
Through from Babylon?

Their master lies broken with fever.
His robes will soon be folded for the tomb,
His breathing as laboured as a slave's.

Nightmare

Night's heavy suitcases fall through my ears and head as I drift to
Sleep: filled with the soiled rags of yesterday and
Tomorrow's opaque packages.

And from the fire of the plane's lungs which spin under
Metal arms the land below is obscured;
The passenger window fills with condensation
Which trickles down the nose of the body.
The beak of the beast too narrow for the pilot to stretch out their legs,
Pooling sweat behind their knees.

We fly through the starless clouds and past the empty
Bone bowl of the moon: the city is far
Behind us; its playground of lights blinking past the jet stream.
The only hope for the shuddering to end is the dive,
And the seers know that a crippled bird is flying to the south.

A dreamer's earnest wish mingles with the fire leaping
Onto the skin, landing on the roof tile of morning.

The brain leaks into a rescuer's hand:
A group gathers to gaze at the orange
Centre of the black box.
They read the position of the liver-grey slats,
An open-mouthed haruspex breathing over the body.

Plum Tree

The men came with their heavy black shoes and
Sweaty overalls one morning,
There to drag the plum tree from our yard.
No reason was given as to the selection –
Something had been murmured about
The slashes of bright red that made even the most fearsome scarecrow
A eunuch of straw.

For twenty or more winters her medusa head
Wriggled its fifty bloodied knots of winter while the birds
Came to pierce and hide in the orbs,
The passive green below washed in uric acid.

The men ringed her with rope
Each one gasping and grunting and looking away
Eventually gaining the nerve to pull harder
As the roots cracked:
The open legs of the branches dragged through the lane and amputated
By the saw's whirling tongue.

Later we lay on the dusty boards of the hallway beside
The huge antique lock of the door.
Our mouths filled with the flesh
Of the last sweet morsels,
Red-stained hands closed around the small hard stones,
The heart of the fruit.

We rolled them silently between our fingers,
Then in straight lines on the floor,
Steering them toward the dirt like marbles.

Garden Party

I have never seen that woman's eyes close:
Perhaps she was born staring

Even when the skin underneath the lids bags
And stretches like a suitcase filled with
Half-glued souvenirs of faraway markets
I am her inexhaustible subject

In between the toasts and exchange of
Terrifying pleasantries she looked away that night,
While the rest of us sang and muttered about the time.

Her lips were pursed as if she was drinking the moon
Through an invisible straw,
Alchemy mixing in her face,
Taking its light like a plump counter of white gold
Into the grid of her lash, letting it slide and fall deep
Within axon and dendrite until it moved deep into the
Bone like a ray:

A flash of leucosis,
Birthing the brilliant dream stone
In a ritual of her own.

St Kilda, 11 pm

Where does hope go when it dies?
Some say it whistles through air moth-like
Attracted to lonely streetlamps which beam
Over needle and
Heel.

Or perhaps it settles on the skin in
Cursed rivers and divine folds, part hopelessness,
Part rebirth:
In the hands of the old man who grips the wheel
Watching the girl twitch under the lights,
The car door sliding, sweaty palms catching urgently
Between legs and polymer notes.

Cycle

The dill has gone to seed in the plastic pot:
Its tired droopy head full of brown pins which I remove expertly
In one swoop, under the purple bruise of an Eaglemont sunset:
The thin sliver of moon tears the sky like a cat's claw,
Releasing a burst of golden star apples
That hang on the bones of the distant tree.

Each seed is a captured world I tell myself, held up once by
A green feathered hand, patiently strained until the fall.
If I must take the role of Atlas it will be temporary:
It was this pot, after all, that bore witness how gravity
Presses its cold grip and leaves the stairs unclimbed,
The thin pastes of cartilage and broken scaffold of spine
Clamped with the same clip that encloses
The misery of a Monday morning commute,
Or a twisted wreck.

The time will come when the globe will balance again on the green,
Away from the weary shoulder and toward the sky.

It is for that moment that patience must grow.
Only this will provide salvation;
Only this will make us breach like the whale.

Indigo

We seek oblivion in hands of lovers and sleep,
Joys clothed in the ribs of the wooden horse.
Though once you have climbed the ladder and looked
Into its large dark eye,
There is only death that stares back – and you willingly succumb –
For is that not what you seek?

Timelessness found in the silence of satiety,
Burial in night's indigo swathes

Looking Out

We do not belong outside this broken window, its frame
Filling the mouth of the termite,
Or even beneath the icy mountain that it encloses.
Yet we dance through the shadows of
Grey meadows in cool slippers of hope, embroidered with the skin
Of our melted heels:

Past the despair
Of the blooming lotus tree which the tongue pushes west of
The teeth, the fruit growing bulbous under the blue highways
Of the eyelid

Milkbar

I remember the time I left the empty house, seven and keyless,
Letting the wind lock the door behind me, in pursuit of a custard powder
As yellow as jaundice at the corner milkbar, the shopkeeper surrounded
By Peter Jacksons and paper bags which he would soon fill
With milk bottles and mints:
The naked straws dipping into syrupy milkshakes at home-time
When the College bell rang.

I crawled back through the window, my head crashing through
The blind like a reverse birth through the labia
Of metal, hiding under the dusty womb of the bed
As I waited for suited Witnesses with grim mouths and gripped
Copies of *Awake!* to leave
Before I could head back to the kitchen,
To stir the milk which thickened and yellowed in the pot.

I silenced my mouth with the stolen spoon;
The brown glass spitting cinnamon on the fatty skin
While the stomach swelled

We didn't buy much more than milk at the milkbar;
A two-dollar note stretched only so far and back in the old country
There weren't any newspapers or gum covered in paper in milk shops-
Only fat custard pies which burned our guts with colic
When the lactose hit.
For we cannot accept that the teat which fed us,
Now makes us cower in the tiny room.

Disability

The heat is an invisible hot fence inside the small apartment;
A worn and brown carpet catches the ash from his fingers
Between the strands of its matted fibres as he watches her
Sweating blond head bent over the scarred trees of
His thighs and feet, which hang off his body
Like abandoned canoes .

Her pale hands wash and dry him as if he were a plane downed
And cracked in some unknown lake-
Carefully,
But without the pause of special attention:
A council ID badge scratches the dark hair and precise scars
With its sharp plastic hand, as she makes hurried chit-chat
About the weather and the weekend:
The only sounds are the swing of her metal and plastic earrings which
Clash with the rush of water
And the wheeze of his breath.
For a moment he is her disciple
Or perhaps her prisoner:
As he stares down at her nurse's shirt which has become unbuttoned
With labour,
Trying to silently make out the shape of her breasts
Following their swell as she moves her arms
Saving the image for later use.
His feet are patted with alabaster towels and he flinches at the accidental
Touches which go further up the dark string of his
Legs when she moves him to the bed or the chair.

He doesn't know whether he wants to tell her to leave
Or cry with gratitude
So instead he smiles silently when she says
I'll be back tomorrow
Her eyes toward the security grill
Dodging the mugs and magazines and bottles on the floor.

He waits for the sound of her car unlocking
On Brunswick Street,
And for the neighbours to flick on the TV
Loud enough to make him angrily wheel himself into the
Corner to rap on the dividing wall.
He tells himself:
It's a privilege to live in silence
As he blows the smoke of his cigarette hard into the air,
As if to fumigate the place

Urban Paradise

They pronouce it perfection,
And she laughs, knowing all too well that the floor is melting into
The ground, making a soup of the grass and soil next to the
Flaking colourbond of the gardens beds, which offer little apart
From clumps of dandelion which shuffle into every corner of the tin,
And assume squatters rights
Throughout the winter and beyond.

Laughter falls from the doors and ceilings and onto the
Christmas table, where the napkins are folded sharply.
Listening like a spider she scuttles when the old woman
Begins to weave a web where spaces
And shapes begin to stick and trap a sigh;
One drawn out and a little too loud, falling
On the table like a funnel-web, scrambling down
Our tops.

The oregano leaves boil in the pot, leaving behind
Their bitter juice in the final cup of tea.
The brew swirls and hot water burns the tongue:
A speck of dirt falls to the base like a full stop.

Memories of The Playground

The kicks of the playground, if well placed, will pass through ribs,
Through the spine's staircase and
A hole will soon grow between the bones and sinew, large enough
For a hand to reach in and pull a lever –
Or pluck a vocal cord - just not so far enough that it snaps
Completely and gives the game away.

Make the body limp and you make it wordless;

The idea is for the hand to move
Deftly, this way and that, peppered with just enough
Positive reinforcement that even the
Lips will seem believably curled, and the jokes will summon
The audience's mirth.

The ventriloquist becomes an ally to the strong hand:
How it labours in the dark of the chest.

Looking for Home

Athens 1922

Look at the sky above the temple tonight:
There's the sparkle of the hero's sword
Its blunted point poised toward the earth.

A misplaced shoe is on a broken ox cart
And the children are weeping in the tent,
Their mouth filled with the aftertaste of
Yesterday's home while they hang the well-worn rags
Between the broken columns in the cella.

A man lights a broken cigarette
Stolen from a soldier's coat:
The tip glows angry red in the dark and
He turns his head toward the west
Blowing the smoke toward the horizon
And the falling sun:

Toward the ghost of the fragrant orange tree and
Jasmine-fenced house which exists somewhere,
Beyond the still of this night.

Low

And although we tried to express our dominion
With the flick of the metal claws which built the farmhouse,
And the pedal of the tractor which stirred the field as
It kicked the dust with the master's blade,
We forgot about the snail
Lying on the flat:

Throwing its silent silver noose around the bud,
Sewing its saliva,
Strangling the stem.

Bushfire

When fire comes to cleanse,
The people release water from plastic snakes
And men in yellow overalls rush through with their metal trucks
Like red blood cells, attacking the mess under the cruel heart of the sun.

Overburdened with the rot of thought and memory
And regret,
The mind becomes an oily eucalypt
That bursts like a fireball in the temple.

And after the splash of address books and phone numbers
And get-well cards dissipates and slows to
Smoke, spring may be slowly coaxed back:

The rain and bird calls which had fled
Will fly to the skin.

Imperfection

There is no greater release than to stand here on the forehead
Of the earth which stirs with mud,
Placing my foot into the mouth of Poseidon's tiny pool:
The broken pipe which has leaked for months and finally broken into a wet
Smile under the ground, like a gum that breaks
With a first tooth.

I fit a finger into the gaps of the melon which still grows on the vine,
The worm-eaten gape of a rotten orange cheek in its bumpy face.
A yellow phonograph horn of zucchini is riddled with parties of ants that
Move from the head to the ground, and lead me to the hidden growths.
Emerald-dark and covered by the vast leaves, a monster head is piqued
By the slashing of the knife,
Growing yet another green snake
By morning.

I used to rake the leaves from the nature strip when I was a child;
Sweep the dirt from the footpath.

Now I look to the chaos autumn will bring:
Of how the soil will shift under frost and leaf
And become uneven.

Hot Springs

We have prepared our bodies to the highest degree,
Parading silently through the mists in our sandals and towels
And carefully plucked legs.
Yet the slippery stones still pinch the arch as we
Fall like naked hens into the kettle,
Staring like Narcissus into the magnesium heart
Of the pool.

A layer of dead skin cells surfaces to the top
Like rolls of cell dough that travel into the
Folds of our bathers.

We touched the seat of the earth, and sulphur filled the nose

Housework

The vacuum moans,
And eats its way through the tiny hills of nail clippings and
Skin and cat hair which have built up in the carpet,
The face bent forward collecting spray into nostrils,
Filling dust bags in the chest.

I'm waiting now for those hands to move
Kitchenward: to chop the meat, to skim the fat,
To mash the potato and have the children's karate belts ready,
For the legs to move kneecap over toe
To the laundry: to place the damp clothes in the basket, ready for the shirts
And underpants to be crucified on the line, high up on the side balcony,
Their fabric arms and legs shrinking and bleaching in the sun.

My palms are heavenward,
Pinning and being pinned,
The peg disintegrating into my eye.

Aged Care

It must be imaginary:
This creaking knee which clicks like the lopsided
Clock on the kitchen wall,
Its hands passing
Slowly over the hunch
Of the number.
Was it really that long ago that we held up the earth in
The palm of one hand?

The foot bends closer to the earth
As each day passes;
The scratch of the worm becomes louder

Enrichment Classes

They deposit us like empty jugs onto the desks which lie
Slick with sweat and the grease of teenage hands
And half-empty activity books.
The lights are low,
And teachers with staring eyes rarely seem to unload the contents
Of brightly polished briefcases.

Twenty years pass, and I am still waiting for the lesson to start;
Somehow it was always chewed up by the clown
Who sucked on second hand gum stuck under the desk, filling
His mouth with the dried saliva
Of the sensitive boy he bullied, trying to absorb
Some of the DNA into his own empty spirals:

Or by the balding teacher who gripped our plaits like chains
Of train whistles, pulling them hard as he grinned with bone white
Luna Park teeth, flushed and excited,
Grabbing his smokes between dirty fingers and blowing the
Plumes into the smooth faces,
His colleague two doors down using the polish
Of the philosopher's beard
And blindingly ready pellets of ancient wisdom to
Pass his number to the girl in the second row.

In the halls we posed and prayed, our hands folded
Like careful wings over navels, the priest blessing the building,
The holy basil leaving its spit on my head.
Our parents later ask for details
Of what we have learned, whether the financial
Investment has been a wise one.

They stand inspecting our virgin exercise books.
Our chest is heavy, the mind filled with the terror of knowledge.

Lemon

I'm shocked by the way you seem to yield to the knife:
The way it plunges into your flesh,
Piercing the wrinkled skin, the tip entering the pores.
You respond with a tear of oil and the sweat of your fragrance
To the violence, more so with that final unnecessary twist
Into the pith which turns your cheek to ribbons.

It is your hallmark to respond with subtlety at first;
Entering blood like a Trojan, pushing your sour spear
Toward the place where bile is made.

Now there is your legacy:
The smell that won't part from the hand and knife;
The acid that eats the table

Lock

The crescendo seemed to scratch the record
While hands slipped like snakes over face and cheeks
Tracing and reading the bumps of her nose and lips like braille,
The same digits which later snuck under the thick hat which sat waiting
On the mahogany hook in the hallway:
Hanging from the brim like a skinned kitten,
Slipping over the brow like night.

Is the crack of thunder over the empty house
Not a melody also:
The parting footsteps dance their echo deep in her memory while
The woman sits quietly by the door, the sun neither rising nor falling,
The world ablaze in her cheeks, light and pitch falling on the
Black eye of the lock

Neighbour

The man was stretched out on the plastic chair
Sunbaking in the driveway of the apartment block on
Trevelyan Street, his
Wrinkled feet shining on the concrete
While pale young boys with their tassels and caps rushed past
Padding their way to worship,
Leaving their grandmothers far behind.

In a pair of shorts and dark glasses, his brown skin was
Held up by rib and clavicle, arms atop his head:
Catching the bulk of the rays
With a pose of defiance, a highlight on the forearm which shone upon
An address or phone number to nowhere:
Blurry digits which had cried themselves into shivers of
Paint long ago: blended and folded
Into the wet telephone book
Of his skin.

This forearm I had seen before, when I was watering the
Garden
Or taking out the rubbish
A branding I tried to furtively read,
Just above the brown leather watch and below the sharp
Fold of the shirt, wondering how little the tattooist
Understood his craft.

There were always melodies of other worlds drifting from his apartment
Somewhat louder during the Sabbath: violins and
The joyful slides of the trombone, jazz and glasses clinking,
The laughter of a woman.

A symphony of oblivion which muffled the
Sounds of the street below,
Yet I never heard him sing or hum
Or hardly speak.

I knew he had died when I found the holy books thrown
Amongst the baby tears of morning dew
On the nature strip that cold May; the ribbon bookmark
Hanging like a still tongue among the
Thumbed pages.

I wrapped them like Moses into my clothes,
Away from rain, and rushed home,
Lest the print should bleed.

Evening Ritual

The time will come when the little boy
Will come into your room late at night
When the curtains are shimmering under the light
Of the wide eye of moon.

Scared of monsters under the bed,
Afraid of the possum that will take him,
Seizing at the breath of the ghost on his neck,
You tell him there is nothing to worry about:
Here is a teddy bear
Here is a hug
Go to bed now

And he patters back
Wide-eyed
Terrified in his bed waiting for the world to become
A heartbeat and warm salty pool again

For he has now realized that the ocean is not only a mouth
For the blood-red sun to fall into,
Or a blue floor for the fish to dance upon;
It is a large tear that spins
Dead men in ships and breaks mermaids
In half.

And you are best to acknowledge
That his pupil has become large enough
To see that there is white
And black.
Or are you afraid that one
Day that same eye may see
You for the person you really
Are?

Orchid

The sickle has fallen too many times:
Sinking its steel under the root
Ripping arteries and veins and white life cords
From the clay which shudders under the rib

This is why the garden becomes a testing ground for the mourning:
The watering can is dry and the snail pellets
Stay in the box
Will you still grow, even if I don't care for you
They say, as they eye the rose which buds on the bush
And carefully space the tender green in the bed as if it were
A heart being placed in a chest
Retreating to watch from the window as the sun
Blazes the plants to pieces

I can only respect you because you grieve with me:
We both know the test is to let the bud fall lifeless in the
The pot,
And to bloom again when the drought peaks
Large purple lips opening to the sun,
Laughing before the raised scissor that threatens the stem

Local Park

1

It's beginning to become dark when my mother ushers me back to her:
She is sitting on the park bench while I play with my school friends,
North of the cannons which sit like iron whales on
Peeling green wooden frames, the ones that were brought back on a
Ship after the Boer War

In that final burst of play before we drop our hands from the swings
And toy wheels of the plastic train, there is a hard slap from a playmate:
It takes a second to register the small
Sting on my cheek and the shock which spreads like nettle on my chin.

The tiny assailant skips off to her father who is busy scooping the
Picnic blanket off the ground,
His back turned to the sky as he ponders ice cream
And a movie

We walk silently back home
Mother's arm wrapped like a scarf around my shoulder

2

Many years later I am walking through another park.
It has been years since I have felt a slide or swing under my body and
I am now a mother myself.

The morning rush has begun but the park is empty

A dishevelled man towers behind me, the rays of the morning
Sun seem to burst from the side of his torn shirt,

And he looks like a mad colossus about to topple.
His words slowly metastasize from friendliness to
Twist and gnarl as the cars shrug the tired shoulders of their frames
Down Elizabeth Street.

We pass through the elms
And magnolias which spot the space around us.
There is no comfort in the floral air of spring.
His breathing has become heavy with intent as he slips behind my back:
Singing of burial under the sand.

I somehow carry the lead of my legs toward the fountain
For what seems like hours, and it is here that he finally leaves me
Under the watery arcs of the Archibald,
To contemplate the phone which lies lifeless
In my hand.
I hover toward the ibis and the little boy who laughs as he chases it
Into the undergrowth.

Later that night I place a phone call to the police at Central.
My fingers press the numbers leaving behind
Tiny specks of water and salt on the pad.
The taciturn constable who answers does not love his job:

'He's been sectioned, there's no more to be done'

My face reddens and tingles.
The words stuck in my cheeks drown in blood,
A sympathetic hand is placed on my shoulder.

Inspiration

Inspiration makes her debut
In empty houses:
Between the clicks of a clock
Or the drip of the tap, though for so long you sought her in
Heaven's starry thunderclaps, your hands clasping
The wide bellies of bottles and cigars.

But poetry, like love, is best made secretly,
In the silence of night

A Trip to the Beach

Somehow we would find ourselves bound for Port Melbourne-
Perhaps weekly-
In the days when the nose of your car would touch the waves
If you parked it close enough.

And there would be an uncomfortable meditation
As we watched the lighthouse stand alone amongst
The swirl
Sitting quietly in the back seat
Trapped by the belt which stapled us tightly.

Were you imagining the ghost ship on the left
Long sunk in the bone sand of Fuerteventura,
Its twin funnels separated and broken
From the body
As the salty paws slammed the windshield?

The car would move to the fishmonger nearby
And later back to the house
Where the fish guts would dangle like necklaces
Over the door handles for days

The Merri Creek

I'm learning to make peace with the mud of the water
That flows through amygdala and vein:
The brown rust flood of electricity
Filled with torn plastic bags which once strained by the tensed calf:
Broken and floating under the nostrils of the graffitied bridge,
Past the scarecrows of the herb garden built on a graveyard of cars,
On the bike trail where the road becomes an upward hill of wood planks.
Merri Creek, or *Merry Creek*, I wonder, as I squash
An old can under my wheels.

And the cycle spins out of control though I am too far back to see:

The handlebars marry with the knuckles of a woman who was
Once a jungle queen, while the fallen boy's t-shirt catches.
He is flung towards the water, caught by a branch,
Swinging gently from the rib like a chrysalis.

His cries bring relief, more to me than him, as he runs towards me,
The helmet bouncing like a giant dark planet.

I'm as calm as dawn

Indolence

When you sit like that in the sun
You remind me of a lizard;
Toothless and untailed
Ruminating over theorems
That exist only in your stunned eye.

You turn your back to the heat and bury your face
Under your hat, while the harvest basket gapes empty
By your dirty feet.

Both stink of vinegar and rot.

How can you tan, while the apple splits and dies on the tree?

The Park At Night

Shadowy figures pace through ovals,
Only to be shrunk by morning sun's radiation
Broken into building blocks of shame, impotent on their own
Smiles and touches hanging like a sore on morning's lip.

Back in night, the shadows rise again,
Billowing black, the gum tree hovering
Over the park bench:
A man packs away the work suit and his children's toys in
The dark space,
His tongue laps his lover's lily ear
Like a cat.

The Shower

The ink of night presses on the jugular like a
Finger, roughly, until I find myself choking at the
Sight of shadows on the unmade bed which glide
Between the limbs and chest,
Grappling before me: ghosts of lovemaking and war.

An empty plate falls from my hand.

Hours later the birds wearily start their song
On the hedge beyond the bedroom:
I turn on the hot tap in the shower, my dark head flopped to the side.
Under the spray the soap loosens my ring, the steam
Throwing its tears on the screen.

Stillborn

We had laughed about the heartburn;
That pink flame which had ignited months earlier, that first hopeful kick
Like tinder in your womb, a spark spreading and
Flushing your face, until you could only sleep half upright,
For hours on end balanced against the headboard like a paralysed
Sentry.

You rose, then sank as if a thief had passed through the night
Of your ribcage.
We talk of knots,
Of her clenched warrior fist and the way it gripped your
Blood in the tiny fingers.
The way it refused to cool, even when the trolley slowly rolled in.

Suicide

The days are becoming smaller again,
Closing in like cold steel rings around your fingers
And ears.

The moths and slaters have hushed too
And all that is left is a wing of a cicada underneath
The old oak and the last few peaches which sag
Like old women's cheeks.

On these nights there is a yearning to
Break apart the wood with the axe
Quietly feeding into the blazing mouth:
You know you can never recreate the sun
With this flame,
So you watch the twigs and bark blacken and
Flake as they flee skyward like flies,
Reading your fate in the ash.

Only when the roar hushes;
When the last ember is free
That is the moment you see that the
Spark has flown and you have burnt the fruit:
No knife will slice it; there will be no jam.

No-Man's Land

We cross at the checkpoint:
The journey beginning with the crash of a stamp,
A friendly Greek smiling at our passports, late of Brunswick,
Speaking to us in a blend of
Broken English and reminiscence.

We hover over green lines and bullet grazed walls where men
With blond hair and baby blue berets adjust
Their arms.

Past the markets of icing dusted loukoumi and carob
Still steaming from the tooth of the ray
The whirl of the dervish smokes through
Like a litany of white planets:

They spin toward the sun in their large white coats,
Each step coming closer to some final destination as
Faces becoming moon-pale in dizziness.

Their hands touch clouds,
The sunset marries our heads

Risk Taker

The sun is very close so squint a little harder:
You seem to have fallen blind seeing black cats
Afraid of shadows in the light
Why don't you try falling in love instead?
That's also a flash of fire
Or lightning: though it may burn,
Perhaps no less that than your safe cup of tea which topples on the hand,
Or the bottle filled with bubbles that rests quietly
In the ice chest:

A knife twisting the top, angling toward the throat

Retro-Movie

A wheel of film as fat as a heart was uncovered in a garage somewhere
In amongst forty-year dust and spider's legs
And to prise the image from the reel with pincers and gloves
Under heavy lights was a type of surgery or magic,
Bringing back to life the forgotten ghosts of 1965
Which doused themselves in the ambrosia of Fosters
And lemon-dipped lamb.

A handsome man plays with
His little boy who stares with eyes as still
As stones, tapping into the pupil of the camera
While the rest of them dance and laugh:
Men in heavy rimmed glasses and women with bouffants
Still dizzy from the sway of the ship.
Somehow these stills are proof that they fought
And ate and loved: without them they are air.

The longer the film plays, the more the dust bellows
And makes me wheeze.
Is it dust, or grey shadows:
One cannot be perfectly certain,
For when the light falls on the screen in a particular way
A figure that I haven't seen in thirty years forms,
Candles and incense falling from his coat.

'Where are my pictures?' whispers my grandfather.
I have no answer for him and he fades away,
Walking slowly towards the darkness, his back towards me,
The way a man shuffles when he has been dead for decades.

Since then, I have flown to his home, and photographed his hat
And his walking stick which sat patiently for years
Under the chair where he died, the cigarette in his mouth burning
As his hands cooled.

His neighbours inspect me closely as I leave.
They tell me I have his green eyes, in between
Giggles and spoonfuls of apricot preserve
And wine.

That night I dream I am liquefying, sinking in dark rooms of memory,
The frontal lobes shrinking like sails in the desert.

Watching Fall

I've always despised weakness, because I never expected to die
Or be a slave to gravity's pull.
But nothing remains of that now,
And I know that past the silk curtain's tassels which dab
The dead flies
There is a child sitting in the sunroom, carefully watching
Me rake the dead leaves.

He listens to the rain tapping its stories on the rowan's head;
He sees the worm squirming in the magpie's beak.

Letters

A ring from the postie's bike and the letters would drop
Into the sandy post-box;
The yellow slot which gaped like an eager mouth from the new brick fence
Which we used to keep the world away from us.

Occasionally the blue and white envelopes would contain
Grainy photographs of
Cousins and death notices which would be displayed for weeks
On the perch next to the plastic clock:
The pictures always accompanied by explanations
Of ages and names in the childish ink loops
Of a relative.

Every now and again there was no use for words:
Under the hundred drachma stamp and envelope would be
A small pack of seeds that customs had missed:

A pinch of lettuce and basil so we could eat
What we hungered for in the hot afternoons
Of the postman's run,
Greece sliding into the oesophagus and stomach, as close
To the heart as we could muster

And our garden would swell with the transplants that thrived and
Died in equal measure, even when the letters stopped coming.

Summer Gluttony

How carelessly the watermelon seed is spat from our mouth,
That perfect black eye round and smooth as
A flat egg hitting the ground and our dusty sandals
Like unwanted parcels.

The tiger stripe shell of skin lies like a frown discarded
To the side; red flesh dripping and smearing,
Hands and tops speckled with sweet summer rain as we lie dozing,
Sated on sweaty sheets, the blinds pulled shut against
The lash of rays and the sounds of hoses
Spraying guffawing children in the face.
Some of the seeds anchor themselves to the soil.

Further away, the melons crack and split
Like expectant bellies in the garden

Tomato

Old before your time:
Lined deep like an old woman's face, tiny hairs jutting everywhere.
And yet you always stand next to the stake
Stiffly held up by a red ribbon or
Torn stocking like the coquette you are, refusing to fall away from
A backbone of splinters.

This is why I love you
And why you repel me too:
Crushing you between my fingers smells of
Poison and sweat and soil,
Your green head nodding in the sun under its sepal bonnet
Slowly filling with seeds, an ovary which holds as many eggs
As can fit on the surface of
A bright red sun, your limbs stretched wide,
Tough and broken.

Exercise

Past the pier at Elwood the runner pounds his rubber soles
Like sticks on the foreshore's drum
Dodging the ice cream van which sits idly on the path;
Its white nose and glass eyes pressing like a giant metal seagull toward the
Joggers and children,
Its belly full of soft drink and soft serve
Squawking Greensleeves from its gut.

He sweeps past hunched couples in slow shoes
And hats
Breathing heavily as he passes them whilst letting the salt beads
Flick lightly off his face.
Reaching the marina he slows down
Enough for me to catch up.
He places one leg on the chocolate-coloured bench and
Stretches;
The tanned muscular limb pushing forward toward the
Faded plaque which is nailed on the wood.
The bench is dedicated by a father to his
Dead daughter:

Maybe they sat there after the diagnosis
As her scalp became shinier and her clothes
Billowed around her as they stared out to sea:
The bumpy golden tongue of the sand murmuring
Something in their direction,
The storm roiling the stomach of water beyond.

It is unlikely that he has read the plaque though:

His movements are quick as if there is no time
To spare, as if his limbs have been possessed by
Aeolus, for he soon starts his familiar pounding,
His legs as straight as masts as the wind pours
Through the shorts.

Beyond the lava black fence that separates the shore from the path,
A child digs an empty bed in the sand with a shovel

My Parents Sitting on the Verandah

They love to sit on the verandah, motionless on the swing,
Placing their own rapacious set of eyes before the large windows
Behind them which lay covered with glasses of lace
And blind.

Their skin has gradually bruised, becoming thin
And creased over the years, just like the paint on the house, while
They overlook generations of ox heart and nectarine which release
Their sweet perfume on the green and brown stalks and sticks.
The ants of late summer march with intent.

Soon they will both move past the verandah and back into the burrow,
Like a weary animal who yearns for the comfort of the dark and
Compact tunnel, retreating into it to begin the final set of
Observations and slumbers,
A negotiation for the ultimate piece of land.

The blood pressure cuff cuts into the veins, the blue estuaries pressing
Those final bursts into the departing white sea of the chest.

I imagine their breath hitting the glass,
The symbols of mist moving past false teeth that
Sleep in the cup, fading slowly into the garden

Lighting The Barbeque

Every weekend he drops a match into the
The dark mouth of the pit.
The black trunks of charcoal begin to blaze vermillion
Under his eye, the lager foaming
In the glass.

Leaning forward to catch the warmth he hardly flinches
When a shower of sparks hits his hand
Like fireballs of confetti.

He shakes the tongs through the glow and watches the fat
Morph into fireworks on the steel,
The white plastic chair creaking under his weight as he leans
Towards the light.

And in the morning the ash will swirl on the deck
The clothes rocking on the line will smell of the past:
Faint brown lines of burn will line his trousers, his finger
Rubbing them quietly away.

Voyage

You say you are on a journey:
A voyage to the deepest ends of the ocean where there is freedom,
Your voice flying wild like the wind-ripped flag on the pole,
Heading to a place where there will be an escape
In the next port or postcode.

The lurch of the propeller
Shakes the summer shirt that covers the dark hold
Beneath your chest:
A cold repository of cars and quiet bikes which lie sleeping
On the hard ground, together with shiny bags of fruit trapped in mesh
Cleaved from the tree by a fast hand,
On their way to the island market.

Stuck next to the sweating woman who vomits her breakfast in
Streams of yellow and white,
The last coffee falls in weak black dribbles
From the crew's kettle,
Just out of reach.

The ferry limps, way past schedule, to the pier.
The ramp falls like a bandaged limb to the ground.

Birthing Tree

In October 2020, an 800-year-old birthing tree sacred to Djab Wurrung was destroyed despite the strong opposition of activists and members of the public

We captured fire from the gods and placed it in the flue:
The choked ventricles of a heater which silently
Splutters the long sleep through a metal throat,
Past the dust balls in the corner of the rectangle;
The heat-bent plastic tiles beneath what is absurdly called
Open space,
When all it does is constrict the throat and char the washing
Suspended over the chair, and no passport is required for the
Rough paper box of its delivery:
Everyone has this poisoned belching cloud in the corner of
The room.

This fire now requires a tented embassy to keep its memory:
Its children fight to save both the body and the story, and
In amongst the jars and pans and margarine containers
The hard face of order appears, twisted pale by monoxide:
Twenty-six days in the cell of Ararat
And even the magistrate wonders why.

Scrapes of bulldozers make way for a loud highway
Hushing storylines of placenta and the cry of hundred-year-old babies.

Under the river redgum the man places his foot on dirt
Strumming the gut of his guitar toward the ground.

Paradise

I recall taking the taxi to paradise once,
The one whose driver coughed his cigarette-laced lungs
Onto the birthed airbag which half dangled
On my lap, its bent head shoved
Back into the uterus of the dashboard with stitches of tape.

I accept his recommendation and we head for the finest beach,
One popular with pale Irish tourists that swirls warm through the Aegean
And marries with the Bosphorus, tracing its way back to Mount Athos.
He tells me that this is where the monks extract its salt for drying fish
That hang limp by the side of their dizzy wicker baskets.

Once there, I'm the only one who doesn't make a sound, hidden behind
Glasses and a sensible rashie on my pay-by-the-hour sunbed,
Watching cocktails and crumpled euros disappearing into the dark
Mouths of cash registers,
Skins being tanned like hides between rounds of volleyball
And the quiet evaluation of flabby buttocks
And carefully arranged breasts.

The lotus of salt and froth brings forgetfulness:
Who knows what going under means?
The dark arm signaling urgently from the wave,
The lung heavy under the peach sun.
It was only the darkness of the sea urchin hiding under the
Rock, pricking the foot, that stopped paradise.

If only for a moment, the blood and needles and hot oil poured on
Brought them to their senses.

Name

Is there a name for this elevation? Slightly forward on the short
Hospital bed, his feet painfully glued to the ends of the frame.
There is a mouth that I feed with gluey oats from a hot bowl,
A final meal carefully spooned into the cold thin arc of his lips.

The window faces onto the palm tree,
Whose fronds have been shaking since he arrived,
And a little further away: the tower of the town hall where he stood in
Fashionable bell bottoms some forty years earlier as his name was
Entered on the roll of citizens,
Though the name written by the nurses in texta
On the walls facing him now is someone else's:

I ask the nurse to fix it through gritted teeth as he drowns in the liquid
Pooling in his lungs
What's his name?
She asks, as I chew my tongue.
He stares at me through the dimming brown

After the funeral we come back to the house.
Mother who has imprisoned my face and name behind the walls
Of her confusion cries for her husband,
Whom she calls by my brother's name

By morning she has placed his photograph on his bed.
I sit quietly by the olive tree in the garden,
The one that casts its shadow onto the empty mattress,
Scraping his initials into the frozen flesh of the tree's trunk, deep,
With my knife.

Midden

A woman and a young boy walk up the hill
Past racing cycles and toward the inverted wood basket
Of Point Ormond.
It is late morning and the ferry has just docked
At Station Pier just over the hill's shoulder;
Their feet move like the rolling waves to their left

She poses him for the camera
And he self-consciously obliges,
Smiling with a lip that's heavy with the first down of puberty

This is happiness she thinks.
Her freedom is sitting on the salt-flecked grass,
Their eyes pointed to the shore as she snaps
Another photo:
This time of a little girl's kite which shakes its tethered
Orange body in the wind.

But it's a mistake to think she is the only one who has found peace here:
Under their legs and cameras and ice creams are the voyagers
Of the fever ship whose yellow flag once fanned the shore.

They lie covered in calico, hastily buried between the silent shells and
Axes and coal of the midden which mingles with the bones of the cook:
Where the ash of the fire that once warmed the Yalukut Willam
Blows hot through the white correa.

Coming Home

A body scurries in the early morning and is swallowed by the office:
Spat out into the coffee dregs of the evening,
Breath steaming white dragons on the bus windows
From the exhaust of lungs.
Our eyes trail invisible links between the exposed globe necklace
Of the beer garden, and the glass peacock tail of the Exhibition Buildings.
The tourette blink of bicycle reflectors and faces are
Washed icon-yellow under library lights which hit the closing eyes,
An army of coats walking sightlessly past us
Through the falling night.

The bus stops under a lamp a couple of streets from home,
About a block away from Curtain Square park.

Under its beam I adjust my buttons severely to the neck,
Inhaling the paused shadow of a quiet bird on the shop's
Pediment, the moon stalking me like a vengeful lover.

Mists

It was the mists of autumn that she would miss:
The spun sugar of morning wrapping around her
Like the finest dessert,
Car's headlights shining like cat eyes, the cardamom and anise
Steaming in the pot.
And finally, the prize, as the scales of fog fell:

A reveal of gold,
Pasted like a gilded sticker
On a canvas of cerulean blue.

About the Author

Maria Papageorgiou-Foroudi was born in Melbourne. She is a lawyer who has worked in community law in diverse areas such as child protection, criminal law and family violence. Published in *Inscape* (1997) and *Antipodes Periodical*, she has won prizes and commendations for her poetry and short stories through the Greek Australian Cultural League's Literary Competition in 2001, 2002, 2005, 2006, 2015 and 2017, the City of Glen Eira's My Brother Jack Literary Competition, and was published in UK *Anthology VSS 365-Volume One-A Series of Stunning Very Short Stories from Around the Globe* in 2019.

Her first poetry collection, *Tears in my Bread,* was published in 2020 (Australian Scholarly Publishing). The book was awarded the Prize in the International Eyelands Awards, Published Poetry category, in 2021.

'The poems achieve a luminous simplicity that is the result both of the experiences considered and of a mastery of language that trims excess and hyperbole...the poetry has eidetic force' - Quadrant

'The poems expressed a range of emotions through understatement and evocative imagery..they have an elegiac tone, conveying life's struggles and losses, while at the same time, affirming poetry's transformative power' - Tom Petsinis, author of The French Mathematician

This book is dedicated to F., A. and C.: in recognition of their patience and love, and to my brother who gifted me my first books. Special thanks to my editor for their helpful suggestions and advice.

www.ingramcontent.com/pod-product-compliance
Lightning Source LLC
Chambersburg PA
CBHW020329010526
44107CB00054B/2035